GALE NELSON

ceteris paribus

Burning Deck, Providence

The author thanks the George A. and Eliza Gardner Howard Foundation for providing a poetry fellowship to support the writing of this project.

Burning Deck is the literature program of Anyart: Contemporary Arts Center, a tax-exempt non-profit corporation.

Design by the author. The cover uses two collages by Keith Waldrop.

ISBN 1-886224-37-4, original paperback
ISBN 1-886224-38-2, original paperback, 50 signed copies

for Lori

CONTENTS

CORPORATE BLESSINGS

great gobs of goose grease

following tie culls

sweat on the
representation of jar

what can felt
reveal to the
sensibility community
that a glass of dry
wine (white) has not
already undone

a severed tendon
accepted as legitimate

a rolled-up rug,
also okay

The modest flats would have been the likely choice for the newly-nicknamed "Monarch Butterfly" of the Greenhouse Society. The saleswoman, who had sold

what is sent from
above/below

theatrical rehabilitation

structured toward
leverage

on speculation
failure
to negotiate

the grid toward
sweetheart

sneakers, flats and sandals to Carolina Barstow for years, was surprised when she decided upon black pumps with five inch heels. The saleswoman, always

diploma knowledge teased
out by charcoal grill

choose to staple the forty-
three page manuscript,
rather than bind

rip lack low

dory flaw

rib calm stir

dot part

turn sod sky

fast with math, calculated: five feet eleven, plus the heels: Carolina will stand 6′ 4″ in these $80 designer shoes. As a gangly teenager, Carolina had been told

what we could use
now is a timid review
of body

torso-ankle relations

a standard two-
row grin of
the entrepreneur

the attractiveness
implicit—the largely
vapid communicated
as though educational

"and here is the other
natural wonder of
the sand pits"

countless times not to slump over when she walked through town, but her mother's remonstrations blew up in their significance once she became active in

fidelity twist
constabulary spunk

ewe jape spa

awn orn

van clay asp

whe sho

financial glimmer
stairwell grid

charities, and thus society life. She instinctively knew that all the other volunteers-qua-gala organizers looked at her as though she were some overgrown

rejection of both
medical types

will she be leaving
today

physical violence within
the orchestral community

two hands in relief,
anticipating rheumatism

and the bitterest words come
from this gloriously friendly
letter addressed as it were
not so much to me but to
itself

face to cloth
cloth to face

dinosaur. She had even overheard two patter about how Carolina was an apt name for someone as tall as a state—perhaps, they ventured, she was

buttress the likely
rival to our contrapuntal
tradition

bet jag mead

squan jum

ger boa elk

sum knack

led pal borne

summons renewal
into his room

mayor as slave
of our enterprise

pristine cowrie
shells

comparable in size to a small country. But Carolina
knew that she was free to choose how she'd respond,
and decided not to fight or get cross, but to celebrate

head to stone for
pleasuring the ears

accentuated front porch

tremble reconsidered when
given properties of proper
noun

tamp down inaccessible
routes to the hill country

did the responsibility
really become too much,
or are you shirking

oh half dime of the
antiquities, come rescue
our latest recoiling
from nickel shortages

her height, to let her forgotten childhood knowledge of happiness *from* height blossom. She quickly built a bridge between her self-image and her height, but

spectacular beltway
and an elderly
man with a
bullet hole ending
his career in
provisions

the rocking movement
catching fire—and
pulling

have apron, will
pander

have geometric
progression, will
salivate

with the enthusiasm
of stripes

reversed all of her cautious, self-doubting thoughts into a curious religion of height. She became a person on a crusade, a Johnny Appleseed for height,

the child in the photo
montage is rendered
in partial collaboration
with its toys

the sudden company
of distention, and in
our own living
quarters

so too the undulating
ski patrol leader, on
break from the slopes

harvest these beans, and
serve them over hot,
steaming goose

amplitude of monetary
parody has never been
the core sensibility
of this literature

scattering good vibrations for the tall-but-shy set,
as though she had become a gardener, tending to
vulnerable, willowy plants.

GRAVITY

for Dani Simons

If, in the later hours toward
dusk, as the energies are released
into embrace, we see each other's
eyes as clearly as you can taste
the sweet young corn
of summer, then we will know
that the force of gravitational
pull is as real as that
of time. And we will talk into
the hours when we have often
talked.

ORIGINARY
PRUDENCE

for Keith & Rosmarie

So that the animal may come to terms with its past,
we give it access to zoological archives.

Dancing bears.

+

The bigger the attraction, we are told, the more
complex the potato farming becomes.

I am collecting the fares this evening.

A perpendicular overleaped by zealous greenery
is neither autonomous nor foolproof.

The coal-eyed ginger cat.

+

Venison upon the topiary commandments, unto this
breviary a well-broken spine.

Specious mandolin adjuster.

"So we come into the restaurant, and see this
kid probably no more than six years old,
crawling under the tables, heading straight
for the kitchen."

+

Ankle-deep in must. A hook half the length
of your inside leg. A pail of sand.

Oh boutonniere, be a daisy!

Egalitarian in the latter days of the regime,
yet unremitting in demanding respect.

The elf regiment in dress uniform.

+

Talcum powder addressed to various parts
of the upper body wounds.

The pocket wench scrubs.

arrival caste

dissembling

chamber complexion

The wounds of our ancestors were originary
in that they could not be predicated.

Alternating between stammering yeasts.

+

When the two vehicles collide, the weight,
speed and intention of impact remain of import.

Jaundiced goal of fifth position.

"The damnedest thing was that neither the chicken nor the child were away from the room for more than thirty minutes without one or the other returning on the run for want of companionship."

+

The selection process undeterred by nominal degrees of avoidance, propelled by vainglorious desires.

I am not your type of singer, I hear.

Inconsiderate belt, tighten away until I
cannot breathe, but don't give.

Sharpened on my headdress.

+

Bemusement meant to relieve all comers
regardless of previous experience.

Muffin gloom.

Sanitized version of the ordeal played
for the revitalization of adventuresses.

The stable is neither full nor beautiful.

+

Chairman, do not resist my loyalty oath,
do not restring my pearl necklace heedlessly.

Spurting ink glimmer.

MEANS TESTING

for Kirsten DeLuca

we mean to mean
he points out
to the brittle group
of well-meaning listeners
the means-testing
embodied by the opinion
makers remains mean-
spirited

the joint hops
when the joint-speaking
engagement
is replaced by
venture capitalists enjoined
from speculative derivatives

no hope for
the faithful
to rejoin
the lapsed numbers

CASEMENTS

Hamlet gung forward the idea of identity
the exclamation to drama great blue eyes sing
the ancillary bellow the forgotten fruit the share

is yours the game blink better the cardinal
to sense a cadaver engrossed jimmy

elephantine specter relieved bong, basso performa

clementine of Kansas ancillary artillery dead in
quest religion for lorn in angst gimble

shame   blunder aware of self's negation

I is we integral bum slay elegant

footwork cut in cloth received as

love gurney-backed authority rescinded
                                        Desdemona, Ophelia, Viola
lever me up
render me loosened

the line is moving toward
reaping the january
the experiment in listening
generously come break press

intuitive engineer oh gloss
camel indifference intellect
gloss glam touch entree gear
samantha fillip constancy
reglow interim pellet goring glum

move on the up
swing of
jump for it
and there is the other
other in the hidden
beckoned tie

that binds
boundary or orb joy

damage oh sorry sorry
lines rekindle the splash
in texture view of samantha
blandishments

sport the plaid and go go
join mark the
space recipient   notion
undertake take take undertake
tie for joke pull-over
splash into a

the sonic interlude is
gracing the recycling
of the curtained chalkboard

    glum   glower speak

gesture yawn
   Intro   go
Plastic toy!

  Go forth   go
curtained chalkboard of
gestural resonance
and physicianal

take   take   take   the better
rendering of dough splendid
gentle description

the splendid distance of the
latterly driven cattle maturing
     is stricken from
these ties
     is stricken from
these ties
     the responsible reasonable underpinnings
spell out the stricken form
into glitter tradition
     in special tone

twe   spa   do   sputt   ga
    stra   ti   ti   cor   cor
        spen

into the dust is a
        cree   tor

into the dust is a

    lee   go   dow

into   the dust is a

            spree-ton-gen

    one

into the dust is a

      grem

  into   the   three

      time

    spor   tum   gub

            stick-wind   GEE
                    five

ENDURANCE

for Matthew Liston

The imperative desire
underscores a leaving
standard unrehearsed
in inconsequent voice.
Sensory corollary
be rigorous in
your leanings as
water waiting
for wood endures
the freeze.
Reserve specificity
for another outing in
and relent to the paddle
home instinct. Savory
twilight, imaginary helm.

IMPASSE
ANGER

for Peter Gizzi

four as one   reliant   come and
you have made   sublimation   grate lemon

The bin resembles aforementioned wire sculpture.

relief   up for bid   shoe accouterment
dismissal time   may we   avenue recline

billeted gloom   cinematic army   done up
integer   if only   these last three

She wants to get the ladybug.

gums   repository stains   folksy dining room
short cut   panning for futures   bleeding

dentist can groove   lax paste   summary
distant   pattern in rubies   only the

Detached from all forms of closure.

you have made   sublimation   grate lemon
four as one   reliant   come and

distant   pattern in rubies   only the
dentist can groove   lax paste   summary

The bin resembles aforementioned wire sculpture.

sudden interest   semblance   but the thing
paid off   glory   ridge in arm

practicum of follicles   grape   transformative design
three leaves   last two chums   gallery

Detour so as to avoid convulsions.

dismissal time   may we   avenue recline
relief   up for bid   shoe accouterment

integer   if only   these last three
billeted gloom   cinematic army   done up

The salesman made three exclusive offers.

paid off   glory   ridge in arm
sudden interest   semblance   but the thing

three leaves   last two chums   gallery
practicum of follicles   grape   transformative design

She wants to get the ladybug.

short cut   panning for futures   bleeding
gums   repository stains   folksy dining room

THIRD PETITE FOLIO

for Catherine Imbriglio

tan hank tor dark tid lare tom
ten tear tod tum
tin hark tire dare -tude lank tam
ton -ture tad tem
tune hare tar dank ted lark tim

confluent segment decay marring
release
jumble

pertain soil

modernist curtain pull embroidery

ladle-cell division consummation

digital stem tiller

replication punishment strobe

time spark sped stank star scare spittoon
stem date tour tongue
tame kennel etude raid rite shark tine
mute dote steer teen
tomb rail tide stark rote gnaw natty

ECONO-
METRICKS

If to build a house
would make you rich

but to tear one down
would make you a real

bundle, then there is
no choice but to raze.

+

Quivering aluminum strap.

+

We sit on a park bench,
you and I, and we talk

as though we were on a
theatrical stage.

+

Red dahlia blooms anew.

+

Produce fewer goods, we
remind ourselves,

but make them profitable.

Making a bunny appear
out of a top hat.

++

The Mexican restaurant comes
into focus.

++

Complicating via alarm
system not, to my way

of thinking, a charming
manner in the urban

or rural setting.

++

The terrace was not
in a fixed location

within the revolutionary
diagram of our fair city.

++

—I sell real estate.
—I sell virtual real estate.

The hangman is unavoidably
delayed (traffic), making

even the gallows party
feel the northerly winds

more acutely than had been
anticipated.

+++

Yes, ladies and gentlemen,
the ace of spades!

+++

Oh joyous centipede, stretched
out to heart's content.

+++

Bicycle tire (punctured)
brought into shop.

+++

Who draws lines with a free
hand has overtaken

each drafting board.

+++

More unreasoned than farce.

Flying squirrels have
adapted well to the

changing nature of
the forested region.

++++

Money lender, heal thyself.

++++

The filibuster will cost
the network executive her job.

++++

This set of plates, spinning
before your eyes, was once owned

by the King of Spain.

++++

—The rate of return dipped again
in the third quarter.
—In spite of what I said in my
column?

++++

Merlot introduced among the
cabernets, easily the most

velvety on the tongue.

Captive breeding program
burthens the public relations

officer at cut-rate
corporate headquarters.

+++++

A jar full of nails,
bent over.

+++++

Steam-cleaned rugs.

+++++

Light fixture broken
in over-extended brawl

during what was meant
to be afternoon nap.

+++++

Flowers hidden up his sleeve.

+++++

The waiter returns
to the table, the

bottle under his arm
chilled appropriately.

Majority, thy will be done.

++++++

We cannot, in good
conscience, cross

that garden path
in these shoes.

++++++

Landmark hotel leveled.

++++++

Sunset not a boulevard
where she comes from.

++++++

—I see them most weekends.
—Must be tough, though.

++++++

The walking on tracks
suspended from the

ceiling induced vertigo.

The bundle was kept
between his knees

as he travelled
at night.

+++++++

Apothecary holding
his sleeve to his

nose to stanch
the bleeding.

+++++++

Moulding beginning
to look distressed.

+++++++

Well worn, that tie,
with its bits of gray

and specks of yellow,
maroon field.

+++++++

Zebra declines.

Anxiety attack leads
to run on bond market.

++++++++

Three cups and two balls,
but the audience is only

apprised of the existence
of one ball.

TEA

for Rodney Cañete

dimbula uva
broken orange pekoe
kandy earl grey

darjeeling dimbula uva
keemun broken orange pekoe
oolong kandy
earl grey assam

dimbula uva nilgiri
darjeeling assam
keemun assam
keemun oolong
lapsang souchong

dimbula uva
uva kandy
dimbula

yunnan ruhuna
nuwara elya
china black
dimbula uva

nuwara elya
darjeeling
nilgiri

broken orange dimbula
lapsang grey
formosa oolong
pekoe green
dimbula darjeeling keemun
assam grey keemun

yunnan nilgiri souchong
uva kandy pekoe grey
keemun

ruhuna nilgiri nuwara
darjeeling keemun lapsang
grey ruhuna

formosa oolong
china black keemun
kandy dimbula elya
yunnan assam nilgiri
grey

ECONO-
METRICKS

Resettled village.

+++++++++

The distance itself
is not at issue,

only its importance.

+++++++++

Bottom is not, I might add,
a reference to sinister

market forces here, but
to your keister.

+++++++++

Computational hierarchy, come
hither with your numerical

progressions.

+++++++++

Pendulum swing.

+++++++++

—I've never required assistance.
—Nor I, but you won't see me
refuse.

It is the stabilizing effect
of bringing the object back

that sends the audience
home satisfied.

++++++++++

Never much in store
for the pier-fishing

set, save for the
occasional visit

from the missionary
school children.

++++++++++

Advances outpaced
declines by a two to

one ratio this
morning, but the trend

was reversed in
afternoon trading.

++++++++++

Predicted nothing.

++++++++++

I prefer ham, myself.

—The porter is near-sighted.
—He's also wobbly-legged.

+++++++++++

When the card cut through
the skin of the watermelon,

the wag sitting next to me
noted that getting it out

would be the real trick.

+++++++++++

Altitude impacting breathing.

+++++++++++

Why not buy in
on the ground floor?

+++++++++++

The holly tree is
without berries.

+++++++++++

Ideogram patterns fitting
a nearly logical system

of interpretation.

Optimal trading down.

++++++++++++

Four different families
have tried living in that

building, but they share
nothing else in common.

++++++++++++

Blindfolded hatchet throwing
with absolute precision.

++++++++++++

Accentual diffidence
bitterly disappoints

first president
for elocution.

++++++++++++

Synthetic ear drum.

++++++++++++

—I'm a player.
—I'm an actor.

Historical anomalies can-
not, in answer to your

question, be taken
seriously into consideration

in advance of their
taking place.

++++++++++++

Bellows anon.

++++++++++++

Trading suspended
based on rumored

merging of
two giants.

++++++++++++

Ah the handkerchief
routine!

++++++++++++

Thematic commiseration
team appointed by the

transition board as
precautionary measure.

—My sources tell me
  everything.
—It isn't what you think.

++++++++++++++

Leotards made for
children based on

market growth assured
in large part due to

bellwether sales
statistics under-

mined by eccentric
shopper known

in town as the
"walking cadaver."

++++++++++++++

Peeling the onion as
an obnoxious metaphor.

++++++++++++++

Getting out of the wooden
box secured with chains

and combination locks.

—Have you got the documents?
—Not so fast, Charley.

+++++++++++++++

A belching.

+++++++++++++++

The vine is cluttered
by the harvester's

tools and gloves.

+++++++++++++++

Predicated on nothing.

+++++++++++++++

Transport in this
vicinity tainted.

+++++++++++++++

Chipmunk avenger.

If I am not mistaken, sir,
tonight is your birthday,

and this is the watch you
were given by the other

members of your party.

VERIFICATION

for Timothy Faulkner

The child is not a thought-forsaken element of human nature. Rather like warm goat cheese eaten on toast is verifiable in the lesser-marked bars of Madrid. Can—as the porous sheet distills—a wave—are you serious about the cap —splash?

Around the bend, we fiddle with coins. Numbness is a constancy.

SHELVING FIXTURES

resplendent in the active way
of coronation planners. the activist
examined his argumentative spectacle
and changed the color scheme
abruptly. plaster the earrings
into the bathing pools, are
recommended, but were drowned
out by the shouts of the
counter-revolutionaries. what could
we do for the crowned prince
but whisper?

anxiety on strings
pardonable excess
charming numericism
abundant largesse fix
sudden silence in a big
frosty glass
arthritic concentration
build the text book thusly
and others amended their bows
sample—glow spew
sharing, gaul spirit
terracing in extremis
solvency excuse
leg   let   spend
  door   door   spew
semb   lack   lad
  tem   tem   put
dove   dove   came
      special   rendering
                  pluck   pluck
                  spume

the subject reclines
      the object declines
                  ampersand consistency
                              movement in

carriageway emphasis
      larger constitutional issues
                  partridge complacency
                              exercise the shattering

a piece of thread

                  spittle cup disinterred
                              floating island summatior

      we journey to the lexicon's
      retreat, and spark a revolt.
                  in the quieter regions
      we journey to the syntax
      center, and placate the sum.

the angle of light has never
been so severe yet we
exude confidence in our driving

we see the exit signs out of
the corner of our eyes and do
our best to keep a steady

distance from other vehicles
severity function is amplified by
our anxiety of serving as judges

in a major competition that may
play out the future for the
participants I am relieved when

the angles shift and only our
ears are super-immersed in sensory
overload

SWALLOW'S BIRCH

for Lauren Acampora

sunlit mission of
architectural faith

birch in shadow
nest spaced slenderly

in lower branches

moonless sky

repudiated adobe

functional breakthrough
miracle of consistency

CRANBERRY
BLUE

Oh dainty feeted lambs

a butterfly the size of
a fingernail

the name emblazoned not on
stone or eggplant seeds—but
in sea foam

greens deeper than muzzles

thrift and iris

"get into the house, Martin"

jumble of pots, overturned

news basket accumulates

spindle cone to salt

wedge mine to salt ore

common mallow and greater bladderwort

In the intermittent passage
between dog-eared and
pristine, comes gregarious
the conversation between

the copious author and
vigilant reader. Who among
us has not wondered at
the state of the book

unread—potential, but
still decorative ornament.
This, then is the book
shelf quandary—how to

yield the contents but remain
a vast field of treasures
to be found by the second
passage through.

Garrow Tor
Rough Tor
Brown Gelly
Kilmar Tor

Brown Willy
Ken Karo
Perranwell
Nare Head

Nare Point
Hawk's Tor
Cripple's Case
Grade

Gew Graze
Pigeon Ogo
The Horse
The Pound

causation jingle in deepest sum

a single divot

proportionate digestion in the
rough-hewn manner of striped
garden snails, kept indoors during
heavier storm warnings

trap-door to dissemblance measure

germander speedwell and common knapweed

Pinch pole replication device, in
action

"that's right, look at the ox-eye,
Daisy."

tambourine clatter entry way

little expectant face, in highest
window

ragged robin and fat hen

Perranwell
Nare Head
Brown Willy
Ken Karo

Hawk's Tor
Cripple's Case
Grade
Nare Point

Pigeon Ogo
The Pound
Gew Graze
The Horse

Kilmar Tor
Garrow Tor
Rough Tor
Brown Gelly

When eating ginger
snaps, please consider
a refreshing glass of
sparkling wine as

complement. You'll find
the buttery properties of
first-grade ginger snaps
to be balanced nicely

by an off-dry glass
of the bubbly. We
prefer that you resist
imitation locales

and stick with
originals—both when
selecting sparkling wine
and ginger snaps.

a brace of nearly three-lobed
clumps

a pitcher for the den

leisure arborist

consequential duct evacuation

period-piece delivery encumbrance

pleasure harborist

blinks and dog's mercury

surround by brown and papery
sheath

extreme variables dot the ovoid

crumble fish rock stating
a welcome

oh pollinated loosestrife

tufted vetch and skull-cap

<table>
<tr><td>We have seen</td><td>Cripple's Case</td><td>Separate</td></tr>
<tr><td>passive winds</td><td>Grade</td><td>the</td></tr>
<tr><td>deter passage</td><td>Nare Point</td><td>harbor</td></tr>
<tr><td>toward inward</td><td>Hawk's Tor</td><td>from</td></tr>
<tr><td></td><td></td><td></td></tr>
<tr><td>caverns by</td><td>The Horse</td><td>the keep:</td></tr>
<tr><td>this coastal</td><td>Gew Graze</td><td>higher</td></tr>
<tr><td>town. See</td><td>The Pound</td><td>middle</td></tr>
<tr><td>then how</td><td>Pigeon Ogo</td><td>lower</td></tr>
<tr><td></td><td></td><td></td></tr>
<tr><td>gale-force</td><td>Brown Gelly</td><td>market</td></tr>
<tr><td>leaves in</td><td>Kilmar Tor</td><td>higher</td></tr>
<tr><td>place</td><td>Garrow Tor</td><td>lower</td></tr>
<tr><td>pictorial</td><td>Rough Tor</td><td>chapel</td></tr>
<tr><td></td><td></td><td></td></tr>
<tr><td>beauty and</td><td>Ken Karo</td><td>lower</td></tr>
<tr><td>an ever</td><td>Brown Willy</td><td>street</td></tr>
<tr><td>shifting</td><td>Nare Head</td><td>to</td></tr>
<tr><td>grain field.</td><td>Perranwell</td><td>church end.</td></tr>
</table>

elliptic course to train the ear
and eye

pin-head sized nut encased in
antiseptic

"abrupt, this frog-bit family . . ."

crestfallen watercress

the amplitude gang in winery mode

eyebright and cat's ear

tufted hair becoming altogether
bracketed

periwinkle tide pool

clever woolen carpet

spatula-eared doozy

stone upon stone, and a housing
development torments the eye piece

viper's bugloss and biting stonecrop

<table>
<tr><td>Nare Head
Perranwell
Ken Karo
Brown Willy</td><td>The nacreous gang, so called
for so many generations
that neither fact nor
legend can explain</td></tr>
<tr><td>Grade
Nare Point
Hawk's Tor
Cripple's Case</td><td>the name, has begun a
fund-raising campaign
for the floating armada
brigade of seven nights.</td></tr>
<tr><td>When nine maidens were met
at Devil's Jump, the engine
descried by scholars was
discharged. Now literature</td><td>The Pound
The Horse
Pigeon Ogo
Gew Graze</td></tr>
<tr><td>found on the case has been
rectified so as to peel back
the veil of mystery that was
tarnishing a good shag pool.</td><td>Rough Tor
Brown Gelly
Kilmar Tor
Garrow Tor</td></tr>
</table>

incidental muttering shire glooms
each doorway proper

drone in three ranges compels

torrenting qua torrent

spin the devices for settled length
of time, to no avail, retrofit
a steel bar, succeed

proper inconspicuous cleft

bladder campion and purging flax

for Emily King Colwell

lumber the distant red moon in
pursuit of its light source

PALLID GLANCES

trade the thump

a piercing

limited view
sovereign

corset of salt

dapper

concern service

survey itself

prod lens

govern screen

renewal chin

neglect in avarice stage

plaque

trace recent

ardent fuse

avail rue patter

fog rat

the lasting

half to quarter
quince

tableture-norming

associate

these three men are
at various points of
starvation—notice
how the one who still
has a water supply
is the most cheerful

supply station
integral device
peddle margin

shield = band

numeral = cup

barter = passivity

austerity rite denied,
ancestry application
pending

This book was designed and typeset in Palatino, New York, Times New Roman and Verdena by Gale Nelson. Printed on 55 lb. Writers Natural, an acid-free paper, and sewn into paper covers by McNaughton & Gunn. There are 750 copies, of which 50 are numbered and signed.